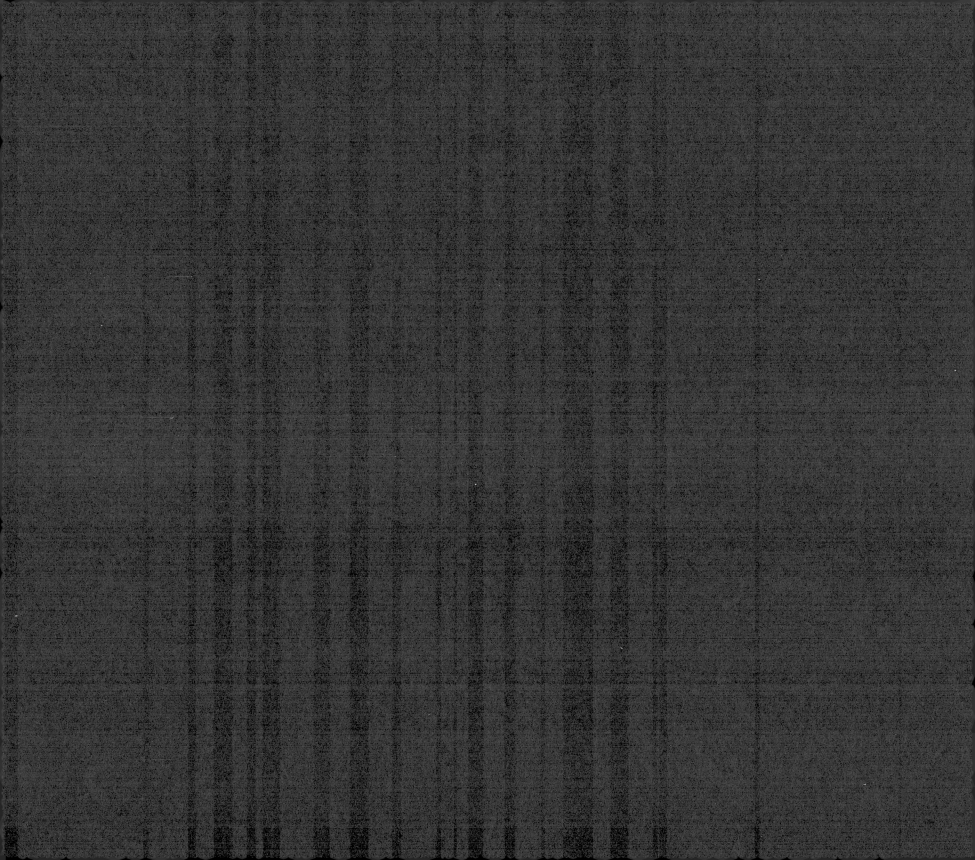

Claude Monet

Published by PaperBall
3600 Las Vegas Blvd. So., Las Vegas, NV 89109

on the occasion of the exhibition

**Claude Monet**
**Masterworks from the Museum of Fine Arts Boston**

Bellagio Gallery of Fine Art, Las Vegas
January 30 to September 13, 2004

Front cover: **Water Lilies**, 1905, oil on canvas, 35 ¼ x 39 ½ in. (detail)

Designed by Nae Hayakawa
Production by Paul Pollard, Tucker Capparell, Motohiko Tokuta

ISBN: 1-930743-29-7
Printed in China

# Masterworks from the Museum of Fine Arts Boston

## BELLAGIO GALLERY OF FINE ART

### LAS VEGAS

## Foreword

In January 2002, PaperBall, a division of the PaceWildenstein gallery in New York, began programming exhibitions at the Bellagio Gallery of Fine Art. *Monet: Masterpieces from the Museum of Fine Arts, Boston* is our fifth and most ambitious exhibition to date.

We are honored to be working with the Museum of Fine Arts, Boston, one of America's oldest and most prestigious art institutions. Thanks to the vision and support of Malcolm Rogers, Ann and Graham Gund Director, we are able to present the exhibition in the unique setting of the Bellagio. Everyday hundreds of people from all over the world come to the hotel specifically to visit the Gallery of Fine Art. Our audience is comprised of wide-range of people from art world enthusiasts to newcomers, many who are visiting an art exhibition for the first time.

The Bellagio Gallery of Fine Art has also become a destination for Nevada residents. The Las Vegas community in particular has embraced our programming and continually inspires us to bring exhibitions of this caliber to the city.

I would like to thank several people for helping to make this exhibition possible. At the MFA: George Shackelford, Chair, Art of Europe; Jennifer Bose, Director of Exhibitions and Design; Kara Angeloni, Exhibitions Assistant; Debra LaKind, Head of Rights & Licensing, Intellectual Property; Kim Pashko, Registrar for Loans from the Collections, Conservation and Collections Management; Dawn Griffin, Director of Public Relations; Jean Woodward, Associate Conservator, Paintings Conservation; Kieran Heffernan, Press Associate, Public Relations; Ellen Bragalone, General Manager, Enterprise; Lizabeth Dion, Coordinator of Rights and External Media Licensing, Intellectual Property; and Nicole R. Myers, Research Assistant in Paintings, Art of Europe.

Special thanks also to Marc Glimcher, President, PaceWildenstein, the staffs of the Bellagio Gallery of Fine Art, and PaperBall.

**Andrea Bundonis**

President
Bellagio Gallery of Fine Art

## Introduction

It is with great pleasure that we present *Claude Monet, Masterworks from the Museum of Fine Arts, Boston,* to the Bellagio Gallery of Fine Art. This occasion represents a new partnership for the two institutions, one that we hope brings great excitement to the residents of and visitors to Las Vegas, and which brings great pride to Boston and the MFA.

The Museum of Fine Arts, Boston, is in a unique position to assemble such a show single-handedly. Boston has a proud history of collecting nineteenth-century French paintings, from members of the Barbizon group to the Impressionists and Post-Impressionists, to the early pioneers of Realism. None of these works were collected more passionately by Bostonians than those of Claude Monet. The door that Claude Monet and the Impressionists opened for the development of art in the twentieth century was significant, as was the vision of those Boston collectors who admired these works and collected them so early on. Some paintings were already in the museum's collection before others in this exhibition were painted, well before the Impressionists had begun to enjoy widespread popularity. In fact, the artist's first non-commercial exhibition was held in Boston in 1892, and his first Museum exhibition opened at the MFA in 1911. In time, and in exemplary Boston tradition, many of those early collectors or their heirs had the foresight to give their collections to the Museum, ensuring that the MFA holds one of the greatest and largest collections of Monet's work outside France.

Just as Monet and the Impressionists redefined the ways in which we see the world, we seek new ways to bring thought-provoking and beautiful exhibitions to a growing audience. Thus, we were thrilled when PaceWildenstein inquired about our exhibiting a group of paintings at Bellagio. Nothing defines Boston's collecting passion more than Monet, and so it was only appropriate to inaugurate our relationship with a show of 21 of the finest examples of the master's work.

**Malcolm Rogers**

Ann and Graham Gund Director
Museum of Fine Arts, Boston

**Rue de la Bavolle, Honfleur**

about 1864, oil on canvas, 22 x 24 in.
Bequest of John T. Spaulding

" The richness I achieve comes from nature, the source of
my inspiration....I have no other wish than to mingle more
closely with nature and I aspire to no other destiny than to
work and live in harmony with her laws."

**Snow at Argenteuil**

about 1874, oil on canvas, 21 ½ x 29 in.
Bequest of Anna Perkins Rogers

Claude Monet.

Camille Monet and a Chil
Artist's Garden in Argente

Entrance to the Village of
Vétheuil in Winter

1879, oil on canvas, 23 ⅞ x 31 ⅞ in.
Gift of Julia C. Prendergast in memory of
her brother, James Maurice Prendergast

" I know only that I do what I think best to express what I experience in front of nature. I allow plenty of faults to show in order to fix my sensations."

**Flower Beds at Vétheuil**

1881, oil on canvas, 36 ¼ x 28 ⅞ i

**Sea Coast at Trou**

1881, oil on canvas, 2
The John Pickering Lyma
Gift of Miss Theodora L

"You know my passion for the sea, I am mad about it."

Fisherman's Cottage on the
Cliffs at Varengeville

**Road at La Cavée, Pourville**

1882, oil on canvas, 23 ¾ x 32 ⅛ in.
Bequest of Mrs. Susan Mason Loring

**Cap Martin, near Menton**

1884, oil on canvas, 26 ⁷/₁₆ x 32 ⅛

**Meadow with Haystacks
near Giverny**

" My only virtue is to have painted directly in front of nature, while trying to render the impressions made on me by the most fleeting effects."

**Meadow at Giverny**

1886, oil on canvas, 36 ¼ x 32 ⅛ i
Juliana Cheney Edwards Collection

**Antibes Seen fro**
**Plateau Notre-D**

1888, oil on canvas,
Juliana Cheney Edwards

**Cap d'Antibes, Mistral**

1888, oil on canvas, 26 x 32 in
Bequest of Arthur Tracy Cabot

This will be something tender. Everything here is blue, ink, and gold, but my God, how difficult it is."

**The Fort of Antibes**

1888, oil on canvas, 25 ¾ x 31
Anonymous gift

**Valley of the Petite Creus**

1889, oil on canvas, 25 ¾ x 32 i

Bequest of David P. Kimball in memo

**Valley of the Creuse
(Sunlight Effect)**

" For me, a landscape does not exist in its own right, since its appearance changes at every moment; but the surrounding atmosphere brings it to life, the air and the light, which vary continually...For me, it is only the surrounding atmosphere that gives subjects their true value."

**Grainstack (Sunset)**

1891, oil on canvas, 28 ⅞ x 36 ½ in.

"What I have tackled is enormously difficult but at the same time of really great interest."

Rouen Cathedral Facade ar

Tour d'Albane (Morning E

1894, oil on canvas, 41 ¾ x 29 ⅛ i

Claude Monet 94

d! This confounded Cathedral is tough to do."

**Rouen Cath**

1894, oil on ca

Juliana Cheney E

"Everything I have earned has gone into these gardens.
I do not deny that I am proud of them."

**The Water Lily Pond**

1900, oil on canvas, 35 ½ x 36 ½ in.

Given in memory of Governor Alvan T. Fuller

have painted these water lilies a great deal, modifying my viewpoint
ch time…The essence of the motif is the mirror of water, whose
pearance alters at every moment, thanks to the patches of sky that are
flected in it, and give it its light and movement…So many factors,
ndetectable to the uninitiated eye, transform the colors and distort
e planes of the water…"

**Water Lilies**

1905, oil on canvas, 35 ¼ x 3
Gift of Edward Jackson Holmes

## Claude Monet

b. Paris 1840 – d. Giverny 1926

Monet's prodigious talent as an artist was first recognized by Eugène Boudin (1824 – 1898), whom he met in Le Havre in 1858. Boudin encouraged Monet to give up drawing caricatures and to paint out-of-doors, which he did in the company of both Boudin and Johan Barthold Jongkind (1819 – 1891). Monet's short tenure (1862 – 64) in the atelier of Charles Gleyre (1808 – 1874) was decisive, for not only did Gleyre encourage his students to go their own way, but it was there that Monet met Pierre-Auguste Renoir (1841 – 1919), Alfred Sisley (1839 – 1899), and Frédéric Bazille (1841–1870). After limited success at the Salon during the 1860s, Monet became a leader of the group that exhibited independently of the Salon; they came to be called the Impressionists, after the title of one of Monet's canvases. Monet chose to live not in Paris but in the suburbs ever farther from the art capital, drawing on his surroundings for motifs. For additional challenges he traveled to the coasts of France, as well as to Norway, London, and Venice. He was a canny businessman, playing dealers off one another and carefully orchestrating his exhibitions and their attendant publicity. In 1883 he moved to Giverny, some sixty kilometers northwest of Paris, and in 1890 bought property there. He worked on the grounds for decades, diverting streams and maintaining a water garden. The area around Giverny and his gardens provided the subjects for his series of paintings of single motifs.

## Sources for Quotes

p. 10: Paul Hayes Tucker, "The Revolution in the Garden: Monet in the Twentieth Century." In Paul Hayes Tucker, *Monet in the 20th Century* (Boston: Museum of Fine Arts, 1998), p. 50.

p. 16: John House, "Monet: The Last Impressionist?" In Paul Hayes Tucker, *Monet in the 20th Century* (Boston: Museum of Fine Arts, 1998), p. 2.

p. 20 Paul Hayes Tucker, *Monet in the 90's: The Series Paintings* (Boston: Museum of Fine Arts, 1989), p. 203.

p. 28 John House, "Monet: The Last Impressionist?" In Paul Hayes Tucker, *Monet in the 20th Century* (Boston: Museum of Fine Arts, 1998), p. 2.

p. 34 ibid. p.5.

p. 40 ibid. p. 8.

p. 42 Paul Hayes Tucker, *Monet in the 90's: The Series Paintings* (Boston: Museum of Fine Arts, 1989), p. 155.

p. 44 ibid. p. 161.

p. 46 ibid. p. 257.

p. 48 John House, "Monet: The Last Impressionist?" In Paul Hayes Tucker, *Monet in the 20th Century* (Boston: Museum of Fine Arts, 1998), p. 11.